The Potato Party
and
Other Troll Tales

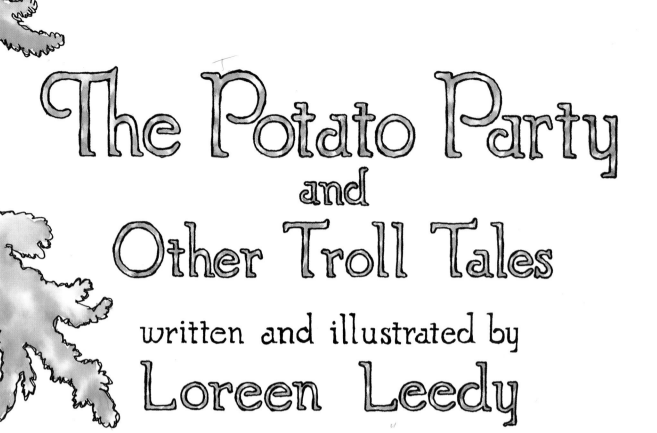

The Potato Party
and
Other Troll Tales

written and illustrated by
Loreen Leedy

Holiday House New York

For Jonathan, Beth, and Sarah

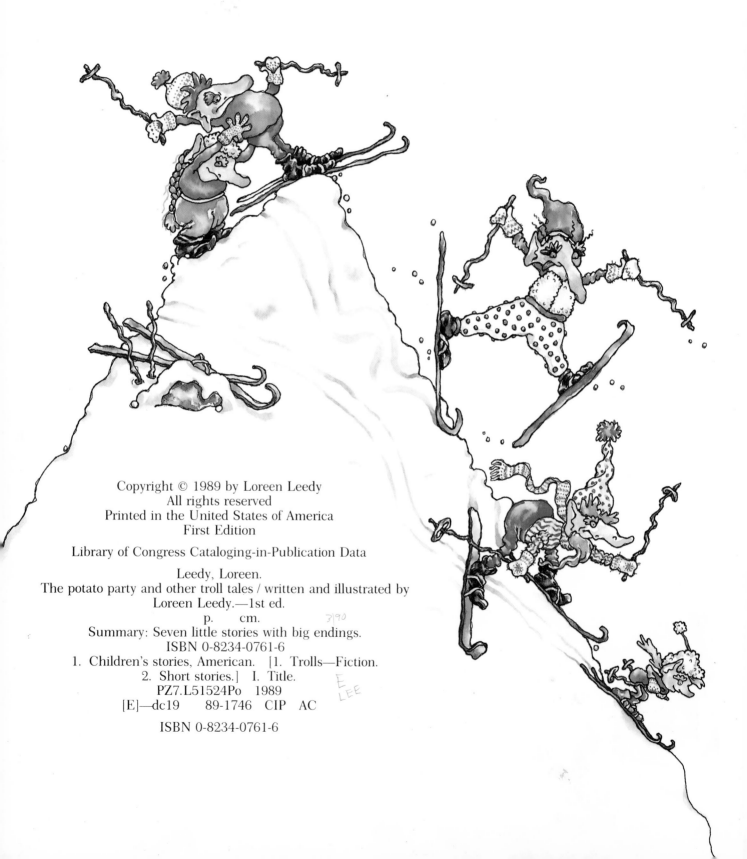

Copyright © 1989 by Loreen Leedy
Printed in the United States of America
First Edition

Library of Congress Cataloging-in-Publication Data

Leedy, Loreen.
The potato party and other troll tales / written and illustrated by
Loreen Leedy.—1st ed.
p.   cm.
Summary: Seven little stories with big endings.
ISBN 0-8234-0761-6
1. Children's stories, American.   [1. Trolls—Fiction.
2. Short stories.]   I. Title.
PZ7.L51524Po   1989
[E]—dc19   89-1746   CIP   AC

ISBN 0-8234-0761-6

Contents

The Perfect Wife

Grog the Proud was an adventurous troll. For many years, he had sailed strange waters and explored new lands. "It's time to get married," he decided one day. "I'll search everywhere for the perfect wife."

He met Hagga at the bottom of a mossy bog. She was clever and owned a trunk full of gold. "She's a fine troll," said Grog, "but the wife of my dreams has a BIG NOSE, BEADY EYES, and LOTS OF WARTS!"

He discovered Dinki on the rocky seashore. She was short and silly and sweet. "She's quite nice," Grog said, "but the wife of my dreams has a LOUD MOUTH, KNOBBY KNEES, and LONG TOES!"

He saw Crabbly on a high mountaintop. She could sing and juggle and dance. "She's special," said Grog, "but the wife of my dreams has a GREEN FACE, STRINGY HAIR, and HUGE FEET!"

There were many others, but none who were just right. Poor Grog began to despair.

At last in a tree he found Grudi. She had a BIG NOSE, BEADY EYES, and LOTS OF WARTS! She had a LOUD MOUTH, KNOBBY KNEES, and LONG TOES! And best of all, she had a GREEN FACE, STRINGY HAIR, and HUGE FEET!

Grog was thrilled and fell to his knees. "Oh Grudi," he begged, "please marry me. Only you are the perfect wife."

"You're right," she replied, "and I must marry the perfect husband. YOU are not him, so good-bye!"

Buggly and the Sleepy Bear

Buggly had a goat that she milked every day. She poured the milk into a pan. Then she stirred, heated, and strained it. By squeezing the curds of milk, she made a big wheel of cheese. She set it on a shelf to ripen.

One night, the delicious smell of cheese woke up a big black bear. He broke into the shed to steal the cheese. The next morning, Buggly saw his claw marks and yelled, "I'm going after that bear!"

"Don't do it!" warned a neighbor. "It's much too dangerous. You will be torn to bits."

Buggly stomped into the forest anyway, taking a bag of food and clothing. Soon she found the dozing bear. She nudged him and asked sweetly, "Would you like some bread and cider with that cheese?"

The grateful bear ate every crumb of bread and drank every drop of cider. "I'll eat my cheese later," he grunted. "I'm so sleepy."

The troll began singing a soft lullaby.
Slowly the bear's eyelids drooped. He
stretched out. He began to snore. Buggly
snatched the cheese and tiptoed away.

She opened her bag and took out a disguise. She put on a big hat, a fake beard, and a pair of glasses. Then she waited at the edge of the forest. Before long, the angry bear appeared and demanded, "Did you see a troll come this way? She stole my cheese!"

"Hmmm . . . stole your cheese, did she?" Buggly grumbled in a low voice. "Let me think. Did she have red hair?"

The bear nodded impatiently.

"Yes, I did see her go by," Buggly said. "It was about a year ago."

"A year ago!" The bear was shocked. "If I've been asleep that long, the cheese is surely gone." He wandered back into the trees, shaking his fuzzy head.

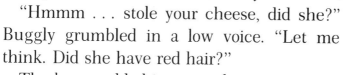

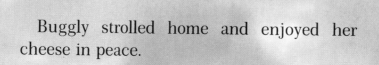

Buggly strolled home and enjoyed her cheese in peace.

The Lamb That Made Mittens

One frozen day in winter, Papa brought home a curly lamb. He told his daughter that the lamb would make warm mittens. Binka giggled and asked, "How can a lamb make mittens?"

The trolls kept the lamb warm and dry, until the springtime sun melted the blanket of snow. Then, Binka led the lamb up the rocky mountainside to nibble the freshest grass. His body grew bigger and his pale wool longer. "When will the lamb make my mittens?" wondered Binka.

Before cold winds blew away the last summer day, the lamb had grown to be a sheep. His eyes were bright, his legs were sturdy, and his fleece was long and fluffy. Binka held the sheep while Papa sheared the wool. "Will he make my mittens now?" she asked.

Mama troll washed and
combed the wool, then
spun it into twisted yarn.

She dipped some into red dye,
some into blue,
and some into green.

When the yarn was dry, Binka rolled it into balls.

Mama began knitting the different colors into a pattern of snowflakes. When the mittens were finished, Binka pulled them on. "The lamb makes beautiful mittens," she said, "but he couldn't have done it without our help!"

The Curse of the Troll King

Murkle and Mog lived in the Kingdom of the Trolls. They were much too lazy to work. Whenever they wanted something, they stole it from the village people. The troll king warned them, "Stop stealing, or I'll put a curse on you both."

The two were caught stealing again, which made the troll king lose his temper. "Thieves!" he thundered. "You give trolls a bad name, and it's time to pay the price. From now on, you must crawl in darkness. If you are touched by sunshine, you will turn to stone!"

"Who cares?" said Murkle. "We can move to the Far North, where the sun is gone all winter."

"Not me," said Mog. "I want to learn how to work."

Grumbling, Murkle left by himself, traveling at night. He hiked further and further, almost to the top of the world. At first, he was happy in the North. He could hunt and fish anytime, because the winter sky was always dark, day after lightless day.

But then summer came, and the shining sun rose again. Even at midnight, it burned like a bonfire in the sky. Murkle was forced to hide in a dark cavern for weeks.

"I can't stand it anymore!" he wailed at last. He carefully crept outside. He moved from shadow to shadow. Then he slipped and fell into a patch of sunlight. Instantly, Murkle hardened into a cold, gray stone.

19

Mog had stayed behind in the kingdom. He always kept out of the sun. During the long hours indoors, he learned to carve wooden dolls. After many months, he gave a dimpled doll to the princess. The troll king smiled as he said, "You are forgiven. The curse is removed. But up in the Far North, Murkle must remain a stone forever!"

The Potato Party

The wind howled through the mountain fir trees as the trolls moped in their cave. It was the longest, coldest, and darkest winter that Tobber had ever seen. "It's gloomy and boring in here," he said crossly. "What's for lunch?"

"Potatoes," said Mama.

"But I'm tired of eating potatoes," complained Tobber.

"And I'm tired of smelling potatoes," added Papa.

"Well, I'm tired of cooking potatoes," said Mama. "But look!"

Potatoes were piled high in a cupboard. Potatoes peeked out of the cookie jar. Potatoes rolled by her toes. "We'll never get rid of them," she said.

"I have an idea," replied Papa. "Let's cook every one of those ridiculous potatoes and invite our friends to dinner."

"We'll have a Potato Party!" exclaimed Tobber.

The trolls hurried to prepare the potatoes.

They scrubbed and scraped and peeled and chopped.

They added butter and cream and flour and spices and salt. Soon the table held platters of potatoes that were baked, boiled, creamed, fried or mashed.

The guests arrived, and they were eager to eat. They gobbled Pink Potato Puffs. They nibbled Sugar-Sprinkled Spuds. They munched Fishtail-Flavored Fries. The troll family grinned as the potatoes vanished.

After everyone left, the cave was quiet. Papa lay snoring, Mama sat sewing, and Tobber sprawled on the floor. Someone knocked— it was one of the guests. "Thank you for the delicious dinner," he said. "Since we ate all your potatoes, we brought over some more. Happy eating!"

The Troll and the Rhyming Bridge

Once there was an old bridge that everyone had to cross on the way to town. When people led their animals over the bridge, it would squeak and creak and crack.

The noises got so loud that they woke up a troll who lived underneath. He poked out his head and called, "Old bridge, why do you screech?"

The bridge replied, "My wood is aching,
It's rotten at heart.
If you don't help me,
I might fall apart."

"Ugh," groaned the troll. "I hate getting out of bed so early."

He found the rich farmer who owned the land. He asked him to fix the rotting bridge, but the man said, "No! It will cost too much."

So the troll complained to the king. "All bridges must be kept in repair," said the king, "or we cannot travel in this land of rivers. Take me to see this bridge."

The king and the farmer stood on the bridge. "The bridge is sturdy," insisted the farmer. He jumped up and down in the middle to prove it. The bridge began to shake and sway.

It said, "My back is breaking,
    The load is too great.
    Please get off now,
    Before it's too late."
But they couldn't hear.

Suddenly the rotten wood splintered, and the king and the farmer tumbled into the water with a splash.

The king was wet and furious. Trembling, the farmer gave all his gold to buy new royal clothes and to fix the bridge. He promised, "Next time, I'll pay for a small problem before it turns into a big one!"

After the repairs were done, the troll yawned and asked the bridge, "How do you feel now?"

The bridge replied, "I'm very thankful
Nobody drowned.
Now that I'm fixed,
I won't make a sound."

The troll scrambled into his riverbank home and quickly went back to sleep.

The Fish Contest

Bomble was walking down the path to the village. Everywhere he looked, he saw trolls with fishing poles. "Why is everybody fishing?" he asked.

"Haven't you heard?" said a big, hairy troll. "Whoever catches the biggest fish takes the princess to the Flower Ball. But don't bother, little Bomble. You don't have a chance."

"Ha! I can catch a ten-foot fish!" bragged Bomble. The other trolls laughed.

Bomble borrowed his grampa's longest fishing pole with the biggest hook. He dug up worms for bait and headed for the water. He got ready to catch an enormous fish.

After a while, something nibbled. He jerked the pole and pulled in the fish. It was only four inches long. Bomble threw it back.

He tried another worm and caught a five-inch fish. He tried again and caught a six-inch fish.

The hairy troll rowed by. "How many ten-foot fish have you caught?" he shouted.

Bomble ignored him. "There isn't much time left," he thought. He looked at the mud that oozed between his toes. It gave him an idea.

He gave the long fishing pole back to Grampa. Then he mixed water, dirt and straw to make sticky mud. He made a big mound and began to shape it into a huge fish.

Bomble dove into a pond to wash off. Then he hurried over to the castle. Everyone stared and giggled. "That's not a real fish!" said the big, hairy troll.

"But it's the biggest fish here," said Bomble.

"You're very clever!" said the queen. "You shall take the princess to the Flower Ball."

The hairy troll frowned at the mud-fish, and the princess kissed Bomble on the nose. She had always liked a smart troll.